DISCARDED

Flint Lake
Media Center

The Doctor's Office

by Gail Saunders-Smith

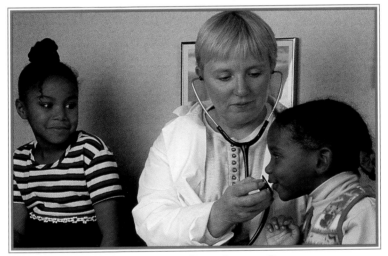

Content Consultant:
Robert B. Kelly, M.D., M.S
Associate Professor of Family Medicine, MetroHealth System Campus
Case Western Reserve University School of Medicine

Pebble Books
an imprint of Capstone Press

1

Pebble Books are published by Capstone Press
818 North Willow Street, Mankato, Minnesota 56001
http://www.capstone-press.com

Library of Congress Cataloging-in-Publication Data
Saunders-Smith, Gail.
     The doctor's office/by Gail Saunders-Smith.
          p. cm.
     Includes bibliographical references and index.
     Summary: Simple text and photographs depict a field trip to a doctor's office, including the
people, the equipment, and the activities.
     ISBN 1-56065-773-1
     1. Medical care—Juvenile literature. 2. Medical offices—Juvenile literature. 3. Physicians—
Juvenile literature. [1. Medical care.] I. Title.
     R130.5.S28 1998
     610.69—dc21   98-11216
                                                                          CIP
                                                                           AC

Note to Parents and Teachers

This book serves as a visual field trip to a doctor's office, illustrating and describing the various workers, areas, and equipment. The close picture-text matches support early readers in understanding the text. The text offers subtle challenges with compound and complex sentence structures. This book also introduces early readers to expository and content-specific vocabulary. The expository vocabulary is defined in the Words to Know section. Children may need assistance in reading some of these words. Children also may need assistance in using the Table of Contents, Words to Know, Read More, Internet Sites, and Index/Word List sections of the book.

Table of Contents

A doctor helps people stay healthy. A person who visits a doctor is a patient. A doctor works in a hospital or a clinic. Some doctors have their own offices. Many people work with doctors.

Receptionists answer the phone. They make appointments for patients to see doctors. Appointments are visits with doctors. Receptionists keep track of appointments on computers. They print out lists of appointments for doctors.

Receptionists show patients to the waiting room. Patients wait for their turn to see a doctor. Children play with toys or read books while they wait.

A nurse tells the patient when the doctor is ready. The nurse has a chart for each patient. The chart lists things that the doctor needs to know.

The nurse checks the patient's height and weight. The nurse also takes the patient's blood pressure. Blood pressure shows how hard and fast a person's heart is beating. The nurse writes these numbers on the patient's chart.

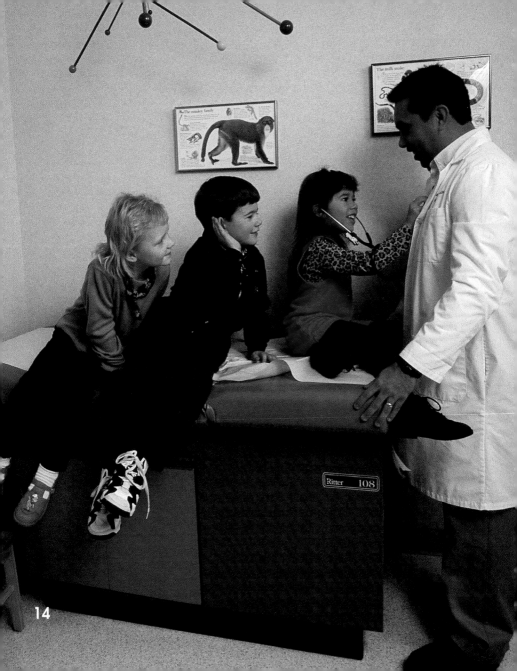

The doctor meets the patient in the examination room. The doctor reads the patient's chart. The doctor listens to the patient's heart with a stethoscope.

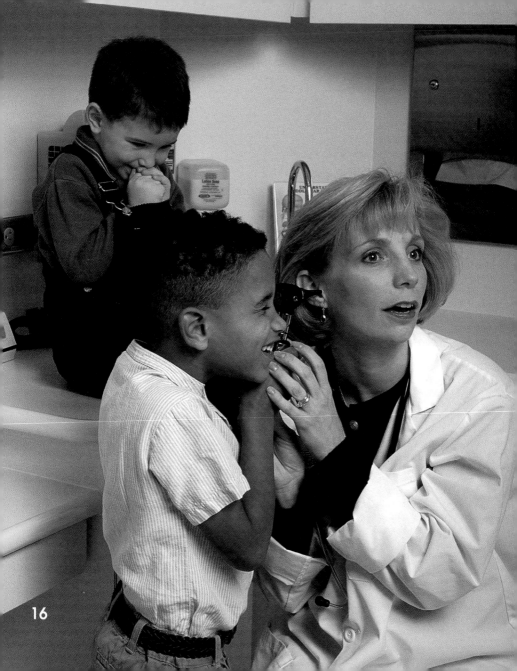

The doctor looks into the patient's ears with an otoscope. The doctor also looks down the patient's throat. The doctor uses a tongue depressor to hold down the patient's tongue.

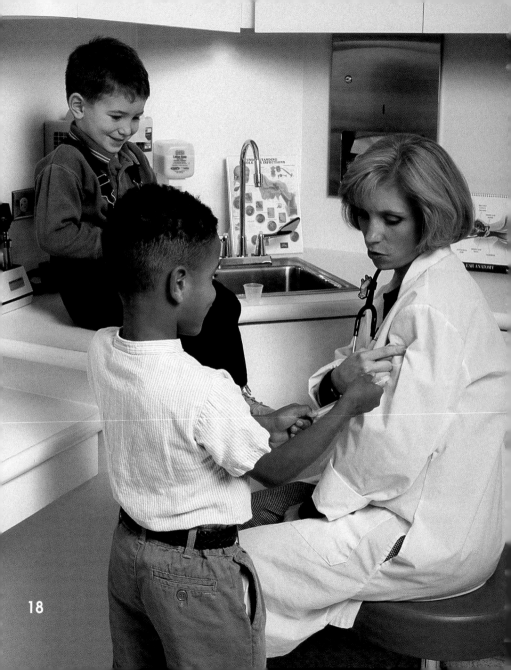

The doctor may give medicine to the patient. Sometimes the medicine is in a shot. A shot feels like a sting. It does not hurt for very long.

Doctors need to know how to make sick people better. They want people to stay healthy. Doctors study books about medicine. They keep learning how to take care of their patients.

Words to Know

blood pressure—a test that tells how hard and fast a person's heart is beating

examination room—a room in a doctor's office where the doctor talks with and looks at a patient

height—how tall something is

hospital—a place where people go when they are very sick or hurt

medicine—a drug that helps sick people get better

otoscope—a tool with a light that lets doctors see inside ears

patient—a person who comes to see a doctor

prick—to stick something with a sharp point

receptionist—a person who answers the phone and sets up appointments

scale—a machine that weighs things

stethoscope—a tool doctors use to listen to people's hearts

tongue depressor—a wooden stick used to press down the tongue

22

Read More

Hallinan, P. K. *My Doctor, My Friend.* Nashville, Tenn.: Ideals Children's Books, 1996.

Johnston, Marianne. *Let's Talk about Going to the Doctor.* New York: PowerKids Press, 1997.

Ready, Dee. *Doctors.* Community Helpers. Mankato, Minn.: Bridgestone Books, 1997.

Internet Sites

Family.com: 365 TV-Free Activites—Doctor's Office
http://www.family.com/Categories/Activities/Features/
family_0401_02/dony/donytv_indoor/donytv079.html

KidsDoctor
http://www.kidsdoctor.com/

KidsHealth-Children's Health & Parenting Information
http://www.kidshealth.org/

Index/Word List

Word Count: **272**
Early-Intervention Level: **15**

Editorial Credits
Lois Wallentine, editor; James Franklin, design; Michelle L. Norstad, photo research

Photo Credits
Barbara Stitzer, cover, 1, 4, 6, 8, 10, 12, 14, 16, 18, 20